THANK you FOR
picking up This Book.
I APPRECIATE your
willingness TO READ
This PERSONAL STORY
AND HopE That it
Changes your liFe !!

VERY TRULY Yours,

Alex Beung
"The Y Guy"

How Divorce Saved My Life

ALEX W. BERING

Copyright © 2012 by Alex W. Bering

ISBN 978-0-7414-7217-5

Printed in the United States of America

Published April 2012

INFINITY PUBLISHING
1094 New DeHaven Street, Suite 100
West Conshohocken, PA 19428-2713
Toll-free (877) BUY BOOK
Local Phone (610) 941-9999
Fax (610) 941-9959
Info@buybooksontheweb.com
www.buybooksontheweb.com

~Acknowledgments~

For the first time in 34 years, I am speechless. Mom, Dad, Adam and Drew, words can't express how much I appreciate all your support, endless patience and your continuous love. You picked me up when I was at my lowest point in my life. What greater gift to know that I am your son.

I am thankful to all my friends who continuously urged me to write this book. A special thanks to the ones that told me to put all my thoughts and experiences down on paper. Kramer, Jay, Vanessa, Eric, David, Vadim, Jasmine, Al, and Mary Anne you were there through my ups and downs and I am incredibly grateful. Uncle Billy and Aunt Dina, without your undying love and encouragement this book would not have been possible. All the good that comes from this book I look forward to sharing with all of you.

The day my son was born was the single most important day of my life. My greatest gift was becoming a father. Much of what I have experienced over the years came as the result of being a father. Alex, I love you with all my heart. You gave me the strength to push forward when I was at my lowest. I encourage you to follow your dreams and never give up.

I want to say a special thank you to Kyle Sheredy for his wonderful graphic design he provided for this book and Dave Shamberger for his continued contributions to The Y Guy LLC's marketing and branding success. I would like to show my greatest appreciation to Marissa who gave me the strength and support to write this book.

And last but not least, a special thanks to Infinity Publishing and to all of the most influential speakers and authors who directly and indirectly helped me. Much of what I have learned over the years has shaped so much of my new found power and influence over other people's lives, is attributed to my new found philosophies, theories and strategies. Perhaps this book will be my personal "thank you" to all of you who have helped make my life what it is today.

~Table of Contents~

Part Two

~Part One~

*"The date is August 18, 2011. Happy Birthday to me…
I am 34 years old and I find myself back in my parents'
house where I started when I was a baby. I'm living in
the same room, sleeping in the same bed, and have the
same bank account. My mother has baked me a birthday
cake. It's time to blow out the candles. What do you wish
for Alex? I wish for………"*

~Chapter One~

"Where there is love, there is life."
– Mahatma Gandhi

The Beginning

I was a sales representative for Liberty Mutual Insurance Company and had been since September 2001. I owned my own home, made over $100,000, had tons of friends, plenty of money and I was single. I had recently started my master's degree, which Liberty was paying for, and lived what I would call a great life. The only thing missing was someone to share my life with.

I was living with a good friend of mine at the time, and he was thinking of taking the next step with his significant other. It was a wakeup call that I was alone. I considered myself a successful, good looking 27 year old and I came from a good family and I was the oldest of three boys. It wasn't like I was trying to be alone, but besides meeting a girl at the bar it was hard to find "the one."

Suddenly like a bolt of lightning it hit me. There I was in the chair at my local Supercuts. She was a salesman's dream girl. I could tell that she could sell herself as a hairdresser the same way I could sell insurance. Honestly who wouldn't want to keep coming back to a beautiful brunette who could hold a decent conversation and give a great haircut?

After about 100 "No's" for a date, On August 19th 2005 the day after my birthday, I got my first "yes." Before long, our dating became more serious and we were comfortable with one another. We had hit that point in a relationship when you are no longer able to keep secrets and the sharing process must begin. "Alex," she said, "I have a daughter. I had her when I was in high school." "Ok, when do I get to meet her?" I asked. I *assumed* she wanted to see my reaction and my behavior before we continued the relationship. My assumption, I came to learn, was correct. If I wasn't interested in children or meeting her daughter, Hanna, the relationship would have come to a screeching halt. Instead, she decided it was still too soon for us to meet and I appreciated her decision.

As the next three weeks transpired, we agreed that it was finally time for her daughter and I to meet. I remember it like it was yesterday. When I arrived, Hanna shied away from me so I knelt down to her level and reached in my bag and pulled out a soft, white little bear (with some candy of course). From that moment, the name Alex was worn out and the father daughter relationship was my first defining role as a parent.

Like a whirlwind our relationship was off and running. We began introducing one another to our families. She lived with her mother in Walpole, right down the street from the house I grew up in. She informed me that her childhood experience had been very different than mine. Her parents had been divorced since she was a child. Unfortunately her parent's relationship was toxic to the point that they still could not be in the same room together. So holidays and family times were always difficult. She had a half brother that was in high school and a four year old daughter. Working as a hairdresser was all she knew. Once she had her daughter during high school, the dream of college was never an option.

Her life consisted of living at home with her mother and working as a hairdresser part time. I, on the other hand, was born in Walpole, MA, graduated high school and went on to a four year college and later started my master's. I also have two younger brothers. My parents are together, happily married and just celebrated their 35th year. My dad worked for the Post Office after graduating from Stonehill College. My mother was a stay at home mom and did not start her career until we were school age. She is now the office manager at her company.

My girlfriend and her mother had the worst relationship I had ever seen not only between two people, but between mother and daughter. I was in shock at the way they spoke to one another. After meeting her mother for the first time, the wheels in my head began to turn and it was in that instant that I knew I had to get them to move out of there. I felt almost compelled to save her and her daughter from the constant fighting and arguing that they were living in.

At the time, I was living in my three-bedroom townhouse with one roommate and plenty of space. My roommate and I talked it out and he was on board with me asking my girlfriend and Hanna to move in. It was a big step in any person's life. For the first time, I felt myself acting on impulse, which for me was uncharted territory. After only three months of dating, I decided to invite them to live with me. My biggest concern was that I wanted her daughter to feel like she was at home. To accomplish this we purchased a bedroom set, pictures, bedspreads, toys, and games. I encouraged her and Hanna to decorate the entire loft in pinks and purples. It was the first time I had that feeling that maybe this was my soon to be family.

I had such great expectations when I invited the girls to move in. Things started off great, but within weeks my roommate who was my very best friend told me that he was going to move out. My girlfriend and he did not get along very well and she made it very difficult for him to stay. I was presented with the choice of losing my best friend or my soon to be fiancé. The choice was made and my best friend moved out. Our friendship of 15 years was broken. I did my best to look at the big picture and the happiness that was about to come. I found myself totally committed to this woman and I planned on making it official.

The holidays were fast approaching and we were invited to her father's house for Thanksgiving dinner. This was the first time I had the opportunity to meet her father. Of course, I was a little nervous, but I was excited all the same. We arrived a half hour late, which didn't surprise anyone in the least. My girlfriend was on her own time clock and no amount of prompting made her beauty ritual move any faster.

When we arrived at the door I was introduced to her father and his wife. My girlfriend headed straight for the bathroom complaining of a stomachache. I was left to field the "late comments" that came almost immediately. Her daughter and I sat down at the table, the food by this time was cold and everyone was beyond hungry. When my girlfriend came out of the bathroom she announced that she was sick and was going to lie down in the bedroom. After she was out of sight, her father with his arrogant tone started our first real conversation.

Father: "So Alex, what do you do?"

Me: "I am an insurance consultant."

Father: "Let me tell you what I think about insurance people."

Me: "I thought to myself, oh boy here we go."

Father: "So Alex, I was at a company and I was making a delivery. I ended up throwing my back out and I was on disability. One day I drove my son to golf practice at the local driving range. When I returned to pick him up he had a few balls left in the bucket and he asked if I wanted to hit a few. Without hesitation I grabbed the club and finished off the last few balls. The very next day I received a phone call from my company asking me to come into the office. When I walked into the meeting I saw pictures all over the table of me hitting golf balls. My disability ended right then and there and I was ordered to go back to work immediately."

Father: "Alex, can you believe that they were following me and taking pictures of me?"

I felt stuck. I knew what he did was wrong, but I felt obligated to agree with him.

Me: "Wow I can't believe they did that."

Father: "Is that what you do?"

I explained that my job was very different because I was the one who sold the insurance to people. Before I answered him there were a million other thoughts running through my head. For instance, people like you are the very reason that insurance premiums go up each year. Of course I couldn't say that out loud, but no one could tell me I couldn't think it.

Thankfully my girlfriend was able to join us later in the evening. I could tell as the night played out that my girlfriend's relationship with her father was just as bad as it was with her mother. Surprisingly, her relationship with her stepmother was heartfelt and seemingly normal. I had never met people like this before. I couldn't wait to get out of there. Clearly this should have been a big red flag, but now I was even more determined to save her from these people.

~Chapter Two~

"Life is not measured by the number of breaths we take,
but by the moments that take our breath away."
–Maya Angelou

The Proposal

Our talks about the future were becoming more frequent. Most of my friends were getting engaged or married and I wanted to be a part of it, too. At 28, to my surprise, I wanted nothing more than to get married. I can remember thinking "How can it get any better than this?" So off I went to make one of the most important purchases of my life; I went to buy the ring. Two carats, the most beautiful ring I had ever seen. I was so proud of my choice and couldn't wait to give it to her. I couldn't wait to be husband and wife. I couldn't wait to be father and daughter. All my dreams were coming true and I loved life and all that it had to offer.

As an insurance salesman, companies have many different contests throughout the year to motivate us to sell more and work harder. The prizes are sometimes trips, over-night weekends, and or cash bonuses. Liberty Mutual put together a contest that entitled the winner to an all expenses paid vacation to Hawaii. The only catch was you had to be the sales representative who sold the most auto insurance policies for the quarter. I worked the hardest I have ever worked to win that trip. I knew that Hawaii was the perfect place to propose, a place so beautiful that it would take her breath away.

We packed our bags and we were off to escape the cold. I remember how happy she was to buy all new bathing suits now that her cosmetic surgery was over. All she wanted for the New Year was, well you can guess. All I can remember her saying was how great it is to be able to, as she called it, "fill out" any top she wanted. I was never one for going under the knife, but I had the money and was more than willing to help her pay for it. I wanted to do whatever it took to make her happy. The least I could do was be supportive of her decision.

In February of 2006 we got on a plane for Hawaii. We flew into Kona International airport. The average temperature was 80 degrees every day. We picked up our rental car and headed to our hotel, The Hapuna Beach Prince Hotel, which was known for having a tropical sunset almost all year round. Our room had a view that overlooked the ocean and was set high above the sand and surf of Hapuna Beach. It offered spectacular views of the Kohala coastline and the resort below. The hotel was surrounded by palm trees, wildlife and tropical flowers as far as the eye could see. The water was a vibrant blue and you could see the bottom for what seemed like miles. During our time there we were taken to an intimate cove where we got the chance to swim with sea turtles. We were able to participate in the Hawaiian culture with a famous Luau festival. That was the first time I had ever seen a pig get roasted in the sand. The hotel planned a hike up the mountains to experience Hawaii's beautiful waterfalls.

While enjoying all that Hawaii had to offer, I had the job of deciding when and where I was going to propose. I remember walking on a beautiful white sand beach with the sun setting behind us. I dropped to one knee and said, "Will You Marry Me?" Without hesitation, she said, "Yes." I figured that she would be speechless, but to my surprise she was full of questions. "How much did the ring cost?" she asked. "What is the cut and clarity, how many carats is it?" Apparently she had read a magazine that told her that I should have spent 30% of my gross salary on it and she wanted to make sure that I did. I was a little taken back and tried to focus on the occasion. I am not sure why her questions didn't trigger something in my brain. Something that should have screamed, "why is she asking that of all things?"

Once we were engaged, people at the resort seemed to be just as excited as we were, our room was upgraded to our very own Romantic Suite and we were given our own Romance Specialist for the duration of the trip. We got invited to take a helicopter tour and flew along the coast of Kona where steep sea cliffs, canopied rainforests, and waterfalls dominated the island. Just when I thought it couldn't get any better I looked down and saw a family of hump back whales.

The week was perfect and I couldn't wait to spend the rest of my life with this woman. In fact, we met a couple who were on their honeymoon and my fiancé suggested that we just get married right then and there. I wanted to marry her, but I wanted my family and friends to be there for that very special day. So we decided to wait. It was by far the most romantic vacation I could have imagined. I left Hawaii with so much excitement and hope for the future, the next stage of my life was finally beginning.

~Chapter Three~

"Success in marriage does not come merely through finding the right mate, but through being the right mate."
-Barnett Brickner

The Wedding

"The day it began for me was the day we walked down the aisle. All our hopes, dreams, and fears are buried in the rituals of getting married. The wedding, the flowers, the fear in my parent's eyes and the state of Florida smiling down on us. Wait, here comes the bride. But something is wrong, were the three strikes an omen?"

Telling my parents I was getting married was supposed to be one of the happiest moments of my life. The reaction I got was less than enthusiastic. Yes, like all loving caring parents, they said they were happy for me and supported my decision. However, they could not hide the looks of concern on their faces. I began to think maybe I was moving too fast. Maybe I should slow things down, but why? I was in love and I wanted to get married. I figured once my family really got to know her they would grow to love her the way I did.

Life was great, my family got on board, and the wedding plans were in full swing. We went back and forth about how much we wanted to spend and how many people we wanted to invite. I wanted a small intimate wedding. My fiancé wanted a huge over the top $20,000 wedding. She had a small family and an even smaller pool of friends. I had an average size extended family, but I wanted this day to be about us, not about showing off with a big elaborate wedding. As we were making the final decisions, I received a letter in the mail notifying me that I won the Liberty Leaders award for 2006. Liberty was going to fly me and a guest to Amelia Island in Florida to receive the award. I was over the moon. This was one of the most prestigious awards an insurance salesman could receive. To earn this award a salesman must show personal dedication to his customers while protecting their financial future. It was an award that honored hard work, customer focus, and sales.

After receiving this information we put our heads together and decided to get married at the Ritz Carlton Hotel on Amelia Island. Our plans were to fly our immediate family down and have a small elegant private wedding. We planned the wedding for May 22, 2006. This would coincide with my award and that way my family could be there to see me receive it. My fiancé was on board, however, I could still sense some reservation in the decision to have a small wedding.

The Ritz Carlton in Amelia Island Florida was beautiful. The dining area was on the oceanfront side of the hotel. We were given a wedding advisor when we arrived and she assisted us with selecting flowers, linens, music, a photographer and a videographer. The hotel also provided us with a priest for the ceremony. We obtained our marriage license at one of the courthouses in Florida. Our wedding planner organized and coordinated all aspects of our wedding. The day of the wedding we were extremely pampered. I played golf and she had her nails done, then we met up for a couple's massage, which took my mind off the ceremony and calmed my pre-wedding jitters. After our massage we headed back to our separate rooms to get ready. I was so excited and nervous at the same time. I had so many things racing through my head. This was forever. I was going to wake up next to this person for the next 60 years. Was I really ready for that? Was I ready for her family? Was I ready for holidays where my wife and my mother would constantly butt heads? Was I ready to take care of her and her daughter and provide them the best possible life I could? Oh I was ready, so I thought.

I'm sure you have heard the saying, "its good luck if it rains on your wedding day." Looking back I would have given anything for a single drop of rain. The day started with my fiancés step mother's appendix bursting. Everyone was in a panic and I thought for sure we would have to postpone the wedding. Fortunately, after a good report from the hospital and her blessing, we were all able to push forward and continue the day in good spirits. After her near death experience we found out that our wedding advisor had quit her job working at the Ritz and that the minister wasn't coming. Looking back it was clearly an omen; like "three strikes, you're out" in baseball. At this point most people would run screaming and who could blame them? We mustered on and were able to get the coat check woman who was a Justice of the Peace at the hotel to marry us. After our vows were said, I felt so happy and proud to be a husband and father to two amazing women.

When the ceremony was over and the hugs and wishes of good fortune were given, I found myself standing there taking in every second of the moment. I looked around at my side of the ceremony site. My parents were chatting with each other, my brothers joking back and forth, and my grandfather on my mother's side was smiling at the sight of me as a married man. As I turned to her side of the family I was jolted back to the present. Parents fighting, and screeching at one another and a bride joining in the fight over who should sit next to whom at dinner. Dinner, a time to feed the hungry, but to me it meant families socializing with each other for the first time. One to one conversation with the other party, mix in a few drinks and you open yourself up to a life time of "I'm not going if they are going to be there." I did my best to smile through all the uncomfortable moments. I can still remember this nagging feeling I had in the pit of my stomach. Maybe it was just the calm before the storm or maybe it was marriage. In that moment however, all this was hidden by smiles and wishes of happiness and cheers of congratulations. As the night came to an end I remember our families hugging and parting ways. Neither family interested in spending that much time in a room together again.

~Chapter Four~

*"The quality of your life is the quality
of your relationships."*
-Anthony Robbins

Reality Sets In

The honeymoon stage had passed and so had three months. I was still adjusting to married life. I learned that my wife was an excellent cook. She made the most amazing pasta sauce, which her family called gravy. The house was always clean and the laundry was always done. She was a great homemaker, and I could tell that she loved every second of it. My wife reminded me a lot of my mother in the ways she kept the house, raised her daughter, and had this assertiveness about her. My wife brought me to a place that I was comfortable. My father saved my mother at one point and I was doing what I thought was the same thing.

She reminded me so much of my childhood that it was an easy transition for me. It was like living at my parent's house again. Little did I realize that you can't and shouldn't try to marry your mother, consciously or unconsciously. As a son, I was a pleaser, and now I was becoming one to my wife. The motto, "happy wife, happy life" was one I grew to live by. I learned that my wife had very few friends and rarely talked to the ones she did have. I on the other hand had many friends that I kept in touch with all the time. She made it clear that now that we were married things would have to change.

I got the sense that time with friends and family could be better spent with her. I found myself separating from my friends and family. The time I spent with her was never enough. The material possessions were never enough. I was working harder than ever to bring in more money to live the life she wanted. My masters program was in full swing and that ate away at a lot of my free time, but I was doing this for us, for our future. With little to no support from my wife, I found my only outlet for frustration was the gym. The gym, however, I was told took too long and I was to stop going. As a compromise I bought some small gym equipment and set it up in the basement. I never saw much of the home gym either.

During the month of August 2006, we found out that we were expecting. I was on the rollercoaster of life and I wanted off. Our relationship was teetering on the verge of disaster. I had just found out at a family cookout that the father of my wife's daughter impregnated her two best friends. This meant that her daughter had two siblings she didn't know about. This was a story straight off of Jerry Springer Show. I couldn't believe what I was hearing. This was not the life I signed up for. The woman I loved was refusing to be supportive in my endeavors to make a better life for us. My time was not my own to manage and I could feel the walls starting to close in around me. I was sinking like a ship. My sales were down at work and my school work wasn't getting done. I had to think of all the wonderful things that my marriage still had to offer. I had to remember why I married this woman, it was for love, right? It was to give her a better life, one that any person would be jealous to have.

After the news that we were expecting, my wife was expecting, too; expecting me to buy her a new car "for our new baby." I agreed that she could use a more reliable car, but of course she said it had to be a Lexus. Not just any Lexus, it had to be the most expensive one money could buy. I purchased her a Lexus RX300 for $32,000 cash. Happiness returned to the household and we were able to start getting ready for the baby. As time passed I came to realize that she had very expensive taste.

I offered to go shopping with her for furniture for the nursery, but she told me that she would rather take care of it herself. I said ok and gave her my credit card to use. Arriving home later that night I saw the receipt for Jordan's Furniture on the counter. I turned to my wife to congratulate her on her findings. "Jordan's furniture had everything I needed", she said. "I was able to get the crib, changing table, rocking chair, and dresser." "That's great," I said, reaching for the receipt. I can still remember the lightheaded feeling I got when I saw the amount. "You spent $3,500! Have you lost your mind?" I exclaimed. She turned to me and said, "Listen Alex, I bought the best baby set they had. My son will not be sleeping on cheap furniture." I realized there was nothing I could do, so I dropped the subject before she sent me to sleep on the couch. A few days later, I came home to bags full of curtains, pillows, and bedding totaling over $500.00. I kept my mouth shut and looked the other way.

My mom was getting excited for her first grandchild, and as soon as we learned that it was a boy she started buying clothes whenever she saw something cute in the store. One would think that this would be seen as a kind gesture. My wife hated it, because nothing my mother bought was from the high end clothing stores; she stuck mostly to Target and Kohl's. My wife, however, refused to take anything that wasn't from Baby GAP, Gymboree, or The Children's Place. My mom handled this well and started a small collection of baby things at her house for hopes of overnight visits with the grandkids. I was getting so excited. I made sure that I was at every doctor's appointment and every ultrasound.

I couldn't wait for my son to be born. I would finally have a little ball player all my own to coach and teach to be a man.

The big day finally arrived. Alex was born on May 12th, 2007. The labor and delivery was a complete whirlwind. Alex was born in 26 minutes. My wife was a professional, I thought to myself. I got to cut the cord and hold my son for the first time. I will never forget that moment and the amount of love that came over me. Who knew you could love somebody that much? Life, I told myself, was going to be great! I mean, what could go wrong? All the pieces were falling into place and life was moving on as it should.

A few days passed and finally our bundle of joy was home. I was more than eager to help with late-night feedings, which I came to find out was a good thing. Already having had a daughter she was perfectly clear in letting me know that this child was mine, and that she had done this already, so he was mine to take care of at night. Sleep was not something she was willing to give up, nor was she up for the "inconvenience" of breast-feeding. I understood that waking up multiple times during the night to feed Alex would be tiring; I guess I just figured she would want to have that bonding experience with him. I, on the other hand, soaked in every second I had with my son. Walking the halls at all hours of the night was more fun than I thought. To her,

this was a punishment for my working so much; to me it
was the greatest gift.

~Chapter Five~

"It is much easier to become a father, than to be one."
-Kent Nerburn

Adoption

My wife was very eager to start the adoption process for her daughter and this seemed to intensify when we found out that we were expecting. I never got the chance to think about how the adoption would factor into other major life decisions like discipline, education, finances and our overall family structure. I know it might sound crazy to think about so many negatives when talking about such a positive event, but looking back I wish that I had taken that extra second to step back and look at the big picture. Was my marriage going to withstand the test of time? Was I going to be able to handle potentially losing my soon to be daughter if it didn't? There were so many questions that went unanswered, and I was starting to become overwhelmed.

But why wouldn't I want to adopt her? I was known as dad since the day my wife and I said "I do." So why was I having so many deep inner reservations that I was struggling to hide as far away as my brain would take them? Stress, I told myself, it must be stress. Or it could have been my family's reaction. I remember when I told my mother. Her response was, "Alex, have you thought this through?" "Thought what through?" I asked. It was clearly the next logical step.

The father – daughter relationship was my first defining role as a parent. I considered myself protective, extremely supportive, responsible and able to provide shelter, food and clothing. I wanted to reinforce her feeling that she was my daughter and she could call me "DAD." So off we went to the courthouse. We were told that we had to file a petition and that the documents that we filled out had to indicate that Hanna's biological father had been an absentee parent. He had only seen her on Christmas day and her birthday and he was always drunk and fell asleep on the couch. He was served the papers to appear in court, but he neglected to show up.

The day of the hearing the judge asked Hanna who was here in the court room with her. She named me as her father and the judge said, "Do you love him with all your heart?" Hanna said, "Yes." The judge granted the adoption right then and there on June 29th 2007. We were complete, everyone having the same last name "Bering" and my wife was happy. After the adoption I felt compelled to read up on psychological problems Hanna might have with the adoption. I wanted this to be a smooth transition for her and I was willing to do whatever it took to make that happen.

The day after the adoption, Hanna and I went out to grab some milk and pick up the dry cleaning. I remember when I was young I would go out with my dad to help him with his errands. Back in the day my dad would pull up to the curb, run into the store, grab what he needed and head back out. Without hesitation I pulled up to the curb, ran into the dry cleaners and grabbed the clothes. As I was paying my bill, my cell phone rang. It was my mother-in-law. "I hear Hanna is with you, can I speak to her for a second?" "I'm in the cleaners, can she call you back?" I asked. "Where is my granddaughter?" she asked. "She's in the car," I said. The next thing I heard was a screaming voice on the other end of the phone telling me "You can't leave a child in the car unattended!" she shouted. I assured her that she was safe and ended the conversation. I was a little rattled after the conversation. I had never had a child before and I was simply doing what my parents used to do. Up to this point that was my only frame of reference. Upon arriving home, my wife proceeded to inform me that if I ever did that again, her mother would call DSS on me. Can you imagine having your own son in law arrested?

~Chapter Six~

"Words form the thread on which
we string our experiences."
-Aldous Huxley

Picking Sides

Life was moving quickly now. Many milestones were about to take place. May 22, 2007 was our one-year anniversary, and my 30th birthday was fast approaching. I had closed the door on one family to spend time with another. My parents were broken up at the thought of rarely talking to their oldest son, not to mention the fact that they were never allowed to see their grandkids. Being a strong woman, though, my mother would muster up the courage to call from time to time to check in.

Around the time of my 30th birthday, my mother called my wife to see if she had any plans in the works for my birthday. Not wanting to step on any toes, my mother thought she would test the water and dance around the thought of a party at her house. My wife said she would like to have a party and would get back to my mother with the details at a later date. Two weeks passed and my mother was getting anxious having heard nothing from my wife. My birthday was in one week, and no official plans had been made. Two days before my birthday, my wife called my mother to inform her that she wanted to have a surprise party for me at my parents house and they could take care of the food, invites, etc. My wife's contribution would be to make sure that I got there on time. I have never in all my childhood years seen my mother so hurt, upset and downright disgusted by another human being. That was the straw that broke the camel's back. This started a war like no other. These two women had detested one another since their first introductions. What is a man to do when the two most important woman in his life have such hate for one another that the biggest room wouldn't be big enough to avoid eye contact? I wish I could say that this all blew over in a matter of days, but of course, that would be too easy.

In fact my wife's father took it upon himself to come to my place of business to let me know that I wasn't being a man in my relationship. He made it perfectly clear that his daughter should always come first in my life, not my mother. He let me know that if I didn't understand that, then he could make it crystal clear for me. My mother-in-law, on the other hand, decided she would go to my mothers work and let her know exactly what she thought of her. My mother was so embarrassed and upset by the altercation that ensued in front of her boss and co-workers. I felt so bad and didn't know what to do. I was torn between my old family and my new family. I knew that my wife could make my life a living hell if I didn't obey, but I also knew that I could lose the love and respect that only a parent can give you. I was fed up and thinking about calling it quits.

A few days later, I received a phone call from my mother's father, a man that I highly respected and went to often for advice. He told me that my behavior and actions were destroying the family and that my mother was devastated at the fact that she couldn't see her son and grandchildren. My family was in complete disarray because I feared to tell my wife, "no" and to stand up for what I wanted. My only response was, "You have no idea what I am dealing with and going through." I was doing the best I could to please everyone, but it was backfiring left and right. My boss was all over me because my sales were lagging. I was doing the best I could with all that was going on in my personal life. My professors were on me to hand in my work and to complete my missed assignments. I was always a great student and I couldn't believe that I was allowing myself to fall this far behind. I couldn't believe that my wife was forcing me to pick between her and my mother. How many ways can a person be pulled before they tear in two?

~Chapter Seven~

"I trust that everything happens for a reason,
even when we're not wise enough to see it."
-Oprah Winfrey

Vasectomy

After a year of marriage, life as I knew it took a turn for the worst. My life seemed to be spiraling out of control. One argument led to another and I found myself a permanent spot on the couch for sleeping. I hated to go home, to my home, the one I bought with the money I had worked so hard for and saved so long for. A house that at one point was all I needed to be happy. Some nights I would drive past the house several times until I got enough courage to park the car, get out, and go in. Just when I thought things couldn't get any worse, on September 19th 2007 my beloved Nana passed away. I was crushed, my emotions were shot, and I was craving love and support from my wife. I began to wonder what happened to the person I married. How do you go day in and day out demanding someone else to live a life that you command them to live?

Threatening was a tool that she used often to get what she wanted. "I am done having children, therefore, you will go and have a vasectomy Alex." "What about birth control?" I asked. "I'm never taking the pill again. Listen Alex, this isn't up for discussion, you will have this done or we will never have sex again." she said. I held out as long as I could, but gave in and made the appointment. It was now the end of October and I couldn't get in till December. Needless to say, she was not happy and thought I had rigged the whole thing hoping she would change her mind. I was hoping, I'm not going to lie. I wasn't ready to give up my fertility. Things between us were getting worse by the second. Thoughts started running through my head. What if I do this and our marriage fails? What if I want to have more kids with someone else? What if I am just not ready to take this step yet? One year into marriage and I am seriously considering a vasectomy, what am I doing?

On the day of the "snip, snip," my wife was bopping around the house like a kid in a candy store. I had not seen my wife this happy since the first few weeks that followed our wedding day. "Have a great day honey! See you when you get home." I was staring at this person in front of me wondering what she had done with my wife. On my way to the doctor's office my phone rang. It was my best friend Vadim.

Vadim: "Alex, I know what you're doing and I really think you are making a very big mistake."

Me: "Vadim, how on earth do you know what I am doing?"

Vadim: "I saw the card for the doctor visit on your fridge when I stopped by the other night. Listen buddy, are you sure you want to go through with this? The two of you are barely on speaking terms. She doesn't allow you to see your friends; people are not allowed to come over the house. You are never allowed to take the children anywhere without her permission and nine times out of ten the answer is 'no' anyway. Alex, your marriage is crashing down around you and the one thing she wants is for you to have a vasectomy. Does any of this seem wrong to you? Think about it Alex, if you go through with this and the marriage fails, you will never be able to have kids again. And I see how you are with your little man, and Hanna, I know that you want more kids. You need to turn your car around and head home."

Me: "Oh my God Vadim you are right. You just said the very things that have been playing over and over in my head. I can't go through with this and she is just going to have to understand."

I thanked him and hung up the phone. As I made my way home I can remember that I was plagued with an overwhelming, uncontrollable bout of anxiety. I was sick to my stomach and feared the worst. I parked the car and struggled to get out. My legs were like jello. I made my way to the door. As I began to look up, I could see that she was standing in the doorway waiting for me. Her smile began to diminish when she realized what I was about to tell her. I struggled to get the words out when she cut me off and told me that I would pay every second of everyday for what I had done, or not done. The look in her eyes was one I will never forget. For the first time, I saw her for who she really was. This had nothing to do with her getting pregnant, but everything to do with me being able to impregnate in the future. It was in that moment that I was done. After that, I put all my attention into finishing my master's degree. I had three days left, and then I told myself that I would tell her that our marriage was over.

~Chapter Eight~

"To be yourself in a world that is constantly trying to make you something else is the greatest accomplishment."
-Ralph Waldo Emerson

I Think I want a Divorce

I had no idea what getting divorced entailed. I decided the best thing to do would be to contact a local attorney that a friend spoke highly of. During the meeting, the attorney had suggested that I bring someone with me when I went back to the house to speak to my wife about the decision I had made to end the marriage.

Four days later, with my father by my side for support, I told my wife that I wanted a divorce. We were both miserable and clearly this marriage was a mistake. I told her that I would be at a three day conference in Boston, so she could stay in the house until we could find her another place to live. I assured her that I would take care of her and the kids financially and we could sign the papers and move on with our lives.

I returned in a few days to grab some clothes only to find her in the house acting like nothing had transpired days prior. Not knowing what to say in that moment, I ran upstairs to grab some clothes. As I walked into the closet I noticed that the bathroom closet was full of black trash bags. I knew immediately that they were waiting for me to claim them. Of course they contained every suit, dress shirt, tie and article of clothing that I owned. To add to the devastation, they had all been shredded to pieces before being placed in these bags. My heart began to race faster. I was furious at the sight of what I was seeing. As I turned to leave the room I noticed a bag tucked in amongst the shredded clothing. It was full of all my personal and sentimental valuables. As I looked closer I could see that most had been smashed to pieces, torn apart or ripped into shreds. I yelled down the stairs, "What did you do to all my stuff!" I was halfway down the stairs before I heard her answer. "I didn't touch your stuff." she said. "Then who did?" I asked. In that instant a voice that was like nails on a chalkboard came from the corner of the room "I did!" My mother-in-law had taken it upon herself to go through my personal belongings in my house and destroy them. I looked at her with disgust and anger. "What right do you think you have to touch anything in my house?" I said. "I will do whatever I want because you are nothing but an asshole!" she exclaimed.

One word that begins with a C came to mind at that very moment, and the second I let it slip out between my lips, my mother-in-law picked up the phone and dialed 911.

The police came to what they considered to be a verbal domestic dispute. I explained what happened and oddly enough they asked me to leave my home! My parents had arrived by then and they convinced me to leave with them in fear that anger and frustration might cloud my better judgment. I was in shock, I had never had any interaction with police before and I didn't know how to handle it. I sat in the backseat of my parent's car in a complete daze over what had just happened. How did I get kicked out of my house? How could all the vandalism done by her mother be overlooked? Fear set in and I began to think that divorce may not be the answer. I was pretty sure in that moment that it was safer to stay with her in a broken marriage than it was to leave her.

We were told that we had to appear in court for a pre-trial hearing to go over the divorce information. This was the first time I had ever been in a courthouse, besides the time when I adopted Hanna. There were so many couples with tragic stories that it broke my heart. This got me thinking that maybe I was making the wrong decision, and perhaps should try to save my marriage. Maybe I was just acting on pure emotion and not thinking rationally about the big picture. As we sat in court, I was instructed to give her a check in the amount of $25,000. I was then handed a document stating that my child support would be $5,000 per month. I was in shock. The figure was astonishing after only being married for a little over a year.

We came to a decision that we would work on our marriage. The attorneys suggested we start marriage counseling. They pushed us to work on our marriage. Maybe they saw something in that moment I clearly didn't. I was thinking about how many times a day I asked myself, "why?" Why is this not working? Why does my wife's family have so much anger towards me? Why am I slowly losing myself? I took a deep breath and agreed to try again. A few weeks later, we started marriage counseling. We would show up once a week, and my wife would agree to listen and be more supportive and whatever else was asked of her, and I would do the same. No sooner would we get in the car, and whatever I had brought up to try and work on she would yell and scream about. Needless to say, counseling lasted all of three weeks; after that, she refused to go, and honestly it was a waste of time at that point. If both parties weren't willing to work on fixing the problems at hand, then there was no point in going.

As the weeks passed, I found myself becoming more and more anxious about going home. I was banned from talking with my friends, and I had strict instructions to be home right after work, otherwise the accusations would start. I was becoming depressed. The signs were all there. I couldn't eat or sleep and I was losing weight fast. My stomach was in constant pain and no amount of Tums could relieve it. Inside, I was desperately trying to ignore the signs, because how could a person like me become depressed? I am a strong person, I thought. I am not a quitter. I don't give up on things without a fight first. I was determined to hide my feeling of depression and work on fixing my marriage.

Weeks later we received a letter in the mail dismissing our divorce action. A sign, I thought, telling us that we needed a marriage reality check. In an attempt to change things for the better, we decided to start over fresh. We stopped talking to our immediate families. We changed all the things in our life that we were accustomed to such as banks, dentists and doctors. Our plan was to "move away" without moving away. So we started looking for a new house. The counselors told us that we should live like there is no one else, so that we only had each other to rely on. The house search went great and we finally decided on a four-bedroom colonial in Wrentham, MA. The house was big and beautiful, and that made both of us happy. The next step was to furnish it. The furniture from my townhouse was not enough to fill a house of this size. We decided that purchasing some new furniture would be a good idea.

On May 17th 2008 we were driving down the highway when the car beside us swerved into our lane and hit us on the right passenger side door blowing out our tire and spinning us around from one guardrail to the other. The car was totaled, I received a SLAP (Superior Labral Tear from anterior to posterior) tear in my shoulder and my wife had minor cuts and bruises. After the accident I was forced to buy a new car. Money seemed to be flying out of my pockets. We were getting ready to close on a half-million dollar house, while buying thousands of dollars worth of new furniture, custom upgrades to the home, and now a car. On Friday the 13th of June, of course we couldn't have picked a worse date if we had tried; we closed on our house and moved in that afternoon. We pulled into a driveway full of delivery trucks holding all our new furniture for our new life. Life seemed to be looking up, so I thought.

~Chapter Nine~

"Don't cry because it's over;
smile because it happened."
-Dr. Suess

You're Fired!

On a Sunday evening just ten days after we had moved in, I received a phone call from my boss asking if I could meet him at another office for some training. I thought nothing of it because I was often the one asked to train the new sales reps or try out new technology. As I entered the office, there seated next to him was the human resource manager. As I sat down, I began to feel nauseous knowing that this was not going to end well for me. A piece of paper was slid across the table.

Human Resource Manager: "Is this your signature, Alex, or your client's?"

Me: "It is my signature."

Human Resource Manager: "Alex, you are aware that it is against Liberty policy to forge another person's signature?"

Me: "Yes, I am aware. I wasn't doing it to misrepresent my client. I was doing what she asked because she was away on a vacation and didn't have access to a fax machine or e-mail."

Human Resource Manager: "I am sorry to have to do this Alex, but that is against company policy and I have to let you go."

As I stood up to leave the room, I remembered how my father and my grandfather instilled in me that it is always better to tell the truth and to take full responsibility for my actions. I knew that trying to lie my way out was not an option. I said I understood and left. Walking out of that room I left behind a $150,000 career seven years in the making, 2,000 clients, my reputation, friends, respect, and my ability to sell insurance in MA. I felt embarrassed to have made such a dumb mistake. I knew better than to do what I did, but I was only trying to go above and beyond to help out my client.

Not only did I lose my job, but the country was headed for a severe global economic recession. Jobs were no longer a dime a dozen. These were tough times, how was I going to bounce back and make the money I was making before? There was no way I could start at the top of the food chain. I was screwed. Now I had no job, a brand new car, a $3,000 mortgage, and a family to support. At nine a.m., I got into my car and drove to the one place that I could clear my mind and think, the one place that in ten years has never let me down. I got in my car and drove to Newport, Rhode Island.

I found a rock on Ocean Drive and sat down. As the waves crashed around me I felt as though I was part of the ocean crashing back and forth against the wall. I was crashing all-right, as far down as a person could get. How was I going to tell my wife that I failed? My fear grew deeper as I thought of her reaction. I could imagine the very look on her face when the words came out of my mouth. I thought of jumping into the water, of disappearing into the vast ocean that lay in front of me. Then I thought of getting up every day and putting on my suit and pretending to go to work as if nothing had happened. I saw myself out in the middle of the ocean in a boat with no oars struggling to get back to land. Seagulls began to screech above my head and I was snapped back to reality. Life couldn't get any worse, I thought, this must be what rock bottom feels like. Looking back now I would give anything to have that day be the worst day of my life. I took one last look around, wiped the tears from my eyes and picked myself up and headed home.

I couldn't put the inevitable off any longer. Have you ever driven someplace and had no idea how you got there alive because you were in your own little dreamland? Well that's how I felt when I pulled into my driveway. The last thing I remember was paying the toll as I exited the Newport Bridge. I walked into the house to a very confused wife being that it was two o'clock in the afternoon and I wasn't due home till after 5.

Me: "Honey I love you very much, I am not sure how to tell you this, but here it goes."

Wife: "What happened?"

Me: "Honey I lost my job today."

Wife: "What!"

Me: "I lost my job."

Wife: "What did you do?"

Me: "I signed somebody's name to a cancellation form about three weeks ago. My company became aware of what happened and they were forced to let me go today. My boss let me know that I could collect unemployment, so I am headed there next."

Wife: "Great we just bought a new house, $30,000 worth of furniture, painting services, wood workers, and landscapers! Now who is going to pay for all this stuff?"

Me: "I am going to find a job, I promise, but until then at least I am able to collect unemployment."

I was emotionally shot after our conversation so I headed to unemployment to see how much I would qualify for. I found out that unemployment would be issuing me $650.00 per week. As opposed to the average $3,000.00 I was making a week at Liberty Mutual. How was I going to make ends meet? Our monthly mortgage payment was $3,000 alone, not including, utilities, small bills, and Cobra. Our standard of living was going to have to change drastically.

When I left Liberty, I was told that I could not take my book of business (all existing clients) with me. I had signed a non-compete clause, which meant that for the next two years I could not contact any of my prior clients. I was left to start from scratch, back to making around $35,000 again. During the next 4 months I was offered three different insurance jobs from highly prestigious companies. I sat down with my wife and went over each one in detail with her. I did this because she was adamant that I be home for dinner every night, she didn't want me working in Boston and taking the train because she wanted me close to home.

Our conversation was far from easy. The concept of insurance, work, and what went into making that kind of money was foreign to her. There were so many things that she didn't understand, and that caused more frustration and more arguments. She wasn't educated in this field and it made it very difficult to explain certain things to her. After hours of explaining to her the pros and cons of each job, she decided that I should take the one that was located in Wellesley, Ma. I had high hopes and couldn't wait to get out of the house and back to work.

My starting salary was $50,000 plus commissions. I knew that I needed to sell right out of the gate to save us financially. On my first day I expected to be out training, however when I arrived I was put in a room with a phonebook and a phone and I was told to call and get appointments for the gentleman who had hired me. This put a bad taste in my mouth. I wanted to sell, not increase someone else's sales. This insurance company specialized in group benefits, commercial insurance, and other plans that I had an understanding for, but was not at an expert level yet. I wanted to wrap my head around the ins and outs of what I was selling before I hit the streets. Making phone calls in the attic of an old house was not going to teach me anything. I looked around the room and realized I wasn't at Liberty anymore.

A few weeks after I started, my grandfather became terribly ill and I needed to help with his care-giving. I took on the sole responsibility for my grandfather's wellbeing when my nana passed away. I always thought of him as my second dad. He was always there for me no matter what I needed. I did the best I could, but there comes a point when one person isn't enough. My wife told me that I should put him in a nursing home, because I was spending more time with him than I was with my family. I decided it was time to sit down with my wife and the nursing home we were considering using. We discussed our options and my wife and I decided to put him in that nursing home. At that point he took a turn for the worse, but he was able to hang on till November 29th 2008, which happened to be his birthday. I was devastated. I felt consumed with sadness. During this stage in my life, with all that had transpired, my grandfather was the only one I was still close with. My home life was intolerable and my job was awful. I was falling behind at work and not making the gains I knew I should be. My boss could see this too and decided to let me go.

A person can only take so much. I had hit my emotional breaking point and found myself bedridden for days. To make matters worse the holidays were fast approaching, we were struggling for money, and the burden for a perfect Christmas lay on my shoulders. I felt like I had nowhere to turn. I couldn't eat, sleep, or even hold a conversation. I was a total and complete disaster. I was so depressed that taking a shower was painful. Depression was more than just feeling sad, it was affecting every aspect of my life. I reached my personal breaking point. My loss of interest or pleasure in everyday activities was gone. In its place were feelings of helplessness and hopelessness, guilt, and failure. I couldn't concentrate or make decisions. As I thought about seeking help, I realized what a powerful stigma was associated with being hospitalized. Death seemed easier, and my life insurance policy for $750,000 would take care of the family. I thought a little more and decided that I was not the type of person who could actually go through with killing myself. I was at the point where I was willing to take on the stigma instead. I had to slow down my brain and silence the never-ending voices. "You are better than this Alex" plagued me daily, hourly. "Why can't people see I'm drowning?" Finally it hit me; the only person who could help me was me.

On December 23rd two days before Christmas, I told my wife that I needed to go for a drive to clear my head. I had no idea that conversation would be our last, as husband and wife. I packed a few things in a small black bag and headed for Norwood Hospital. Thoughts of suicide had consumed me, and I knew that if I stayed in that house for another second I might do harm to myself. I was scared, but knew the choice I was making was the right one. I was issued a room and a psychologist. I picked up the phone in the hallway, and with a heavy heart I called my dad. I hadn't spoken to my family in nine months. I told him where I was and that I was sorry. My parents arrived at my bedside in what seemed like minutes, with love and fear in their eyes. Never in their lives could they have imagined anything like this happening to me, or any of their children. They were unprepared emotionally for the months that were to follow.

I told my doctor that thousands of thoughts pass through my mind daily. I explained that when I lay my head down on the pillow that is where 100's of thousands of thoughts race through me. "Unfortunately we only retain a few and most are forgotten forever," said the doctor. He recommended that I sleep with a pen and piece of paper next to my bed. That one suggestion helped me to cure my insomnia. During my stay at the hospital, I was given the diagnosis of Situational Depression. Situational Depression is considered an adjustment disorder rather than a true depression. Emotional and behavioral symptoms reduced my normal functioning. I was under constant observation; there was a daily routine that was flexible. This was the time I had to think about myself. I came to the conclusion that I needed help.

I needed to drop out of the game of life for a while. I had to put life, success, children on hold. My doctor was educating me on why I was suffering so deeply. He told me that the loss of two loved ones, loss of a job, loss of a relationship, and the experience of a traumatic event had affected my quality of life. Coping skills, breathing techniques, and medications helped manage my negative emotions. My doctor suggested that I go away for a while and leave behind all the things that were making life so unlivable. I called my uncle who lived in Colorado and asked if I could stay with him for a while. My doctor had suggested a great medical practice there, which would allow me to finish my therapy. After the "ok" from my Aunt and Uncle, I checked myself out on January 1st 2009 and headed to Colorado. Medication, therapy, and a therapeutic environment were awaiting me when I arrived. My uncle didn't even recognize me. I was so thin and my face had a look of pain and exhaustion. With the help of doctors and my family, I got back structure, strength, and a sound mind. It removed me from my home environment of stress and anxiety.

~Chapter Ten~

"There is a saying in Tibetan, 'Tragedy should be utilized as a source of strength.' No matter what sort of difficulties, how painful experience is, if we lose our hope, that's our real disaster."
-Dalai Lama XIV

A Place to Clear My Head

While in Colorado, I questioned everything I did. I wanted to make sure that I made the right decision to leave, to escape for a month, the life that was killing me. My mission was to return strong enough mentally and physically to confront my marriage and the past. I kept reminding myself that I had no choice; it was doctor's orders. My uncle and I created a daily schedule that I could follow. I would wake up, look for jobs, speak with different attorneys, then I would go to the gym, attend my hour meetings with the councilor and then dinner with the family.

Moving to Colorado gave me the opportunity to take a break, and catch my breath. My counselor, told me to create a time line of the biggest jobs, projects, and roadblocks that affected me mentally. My uncle was a huge help. He got me reading books on psychology, depression, and human behavior. I became addicted to learning about myself and what I was going through. My uncle worked for a company that linked human behavior to job behavior. I was fascinated by what he did, and it got the wheels in my head turning. The more information I got about human behavior, the more I understood what was happening to me and my relationship with my wife. I was finally confident that I was making the right decision in getting divorced. The week before I left to return to Massachusetts, my counselor suggested that I finally pick an attorney. He wanted to make sure that most of the big decisions were made before I left so that I would not be overwhelmed when I returned. I found my attorney and was educated on how an initial filing had to be done, which would lead to the division of assets, alimony, child support, custody, and lastly, visitation. I told my new attorney that my goal here was to preserve my sanity.

Before leaving Colorado I received mail that my parents had forwarded to me. It contained a letter from the Massachusetts Division of Insurance regarding an investigation. The letter stated that the Division has cause to believe that I may have violated the Massachusetts insurance laws. Once I read through the letter, I learned that when Liberty let me go, they were then required to notify the state of my actions. This put me under investigation, and my insurance licenses in jeopardy. I was asked to appear in court for a hearing. I notified the court that I was in Colorado on doctor's orders and could not make the scheduled court date. They told me that I could pay a $1,000 fine and write a letter stating why I did what I did and what I learned from my behavior to settle the case. My uncle and I sat down and completed the letter for the court and my parents came up with the money for the fine. The court read my letter and decided that I did not do anything with malicious intent or to better myself financially. The investigation was dropped and my licenses were reinstated.

I spoke with my parents and we decided that instead of staying with them, that it would be best if I went to stay with my childhood friends in Worcester, MA. I agreed, baby steps are what I needed. I don't think I could have jumped right back into reality and the chance of bumping into people I knew. I wasn't ready for that yet. So instead I decided to stay with my friends Jay and Vanessa for a month and a half in Worcester.

While I was there I was given the opportunity to take part in a depression study. I had little to no money. My health insurance had run out right before I left

Colorado, so I had no way to pay for the medication they had me on. The study I was considering taking part in was run by Boston Clinical Trials. I found out that I would receive a hundred dollars a week, and frankly I was willing to try anything to feel better. All I had to do was give blood, urine, and weight. Some portions of the study required me to take computer tests. Only the company that was doing the study knew if I was on an actual medication or on a placebo. I didn't think I was getting any better; I really felt like there was no medication out there in the world that could help me. I was in a place where I couldn't remember what I had for breakfast, let alone how I felt on or off medication. One of the perks was that I received free counseling while taking part in the study. This helped, and allowed me the time I needed to make the official transition home to my parent's house.

~Chapter Eleven~

"Whenever you set out to do something,
something else must be done first."
-Murphy's Law

House for Sale

Upon returning home to my parent's house, I decided to drive by my house to see what shape it was in. I hadn't seen it in two and a half months. As I drove by, I saw multiple cars in the drive way belonging to my soon to be ex-wife's family members. All her family and friends were now living in my house. I couldn't believe it. I would say I was shocked, but nothing shocked me anymore. I got back to my parent's house and notified my attorney that my wife was housing her entire family in my house and that I think we should get it on the market as soon as possible. I also notified her that I was still being denied visitation with my children. My attorney said that she would do her best to get me my visitation with my children.

After weeks of not allowing me to see my children, I finally got the ok to come to the house and pick up Alex for a scheduled visitation. I was unable to take Hanna because she was in school. On April 29th, 2009 I was excited at the thought of seeing my little man, but fear had set in, making me extremely nervous and anxious. I entered the house and headed straight for the bedroom to grab Alex and some diapers. As I headed for the door she stopped me and told me that I couldn't take the diapers. I told her that I didn't have enough time to grab some on my way over and I would replace them when I brought him back. As she moved towards the kitchen I headed for my car. My wife began screaming and threatening to call the cops if I left with the diapers. By this time I was already putting Alex in his car seat. She began screaming at me on the front lawn. I told her that I had a scheduled visitation and I would bring Alex and some diapers back when it was over. As I drove away my cell phone began to ring, it was her. I refused to answer it and so she continued to call six more times. In the mean time she decided to call the Wrentham police and tell them that I grabbed her arm and hurt her when I was leaving the house with Alex. I later got a voice message from the Wrentham police department, looking to arrest me on charges of assault and battery. I didn't know what to do so I called my mom because she knew a lot of Walpole policemen. She advised me to call a family friend who was a local police officer.

He suggested that I go and stay at a friend's house because it was a long holiday weekend and I would be sitting in a jail cell for three days if I went to the station. I made my decision and dropped Alex off to my mom and headed back to Worcester, MA. Mom and Dad brought Alex back at the scheduled time. As soon as I got to Worcester, I contacted an attorney and hired him for $10,000 to represent me. He told me that he would turn me into the Wrentham court house on Tuesday morning. My wife did her best to paint a picture of mental illness and fear for her life. The courts, however, found me innocent and dismissed the criminal matter and restraining order.

A few weeks later on May 12th I went to the police station (the pickups and drop offs had been moved there to make sure that no party involved was harmed in any way during the handing off of the children) to pick up Alex for my scheduled visitation. Up to this point all the visitation had been scheduled week by week by our attorney's. May 12th also happened to be Alex's second birthday. I was all excited. We had a party and family members back at my parent's house waiting for him. My parents and I waited in the car for 30 minutes and, of course, my ex-wife was a no show. I was completely heartbroken. I went into the police station to file one of many police reports.

I was in close contact with my divorce attorney at this point and she told me that it would be in my better interest, if I could handle it, to find a job. I started interviewing and was able to get a job selling cable, internet and phone packages for Comcast. My attorney told me it would help me in court because child support was going to kick in and, frankly, having a little income and something to do everyday couldn't hurt either. My attorney contacted my wife's attorney and they agreed that we had to sell the house because neither one of us could afford to live there. I was told that I had to pay all the expenses to keep the house running until we were able to sell it. My wife was told that she had to be flexible for showings and she had to keep the appearance of the house up, looking good inside and out.

Not having any money left I was forced to liquidate all my assets. I wiped out my 401K and any retirement plans that I set up with Liberty Mutual. The average monthly cost that I had to come up with was around $6,000. I received $107,000 from my 401K and around $62,000 from the rest. The rest of the money was slowly eaten away every month by bills. Our house was on the market from March of 2009 to September of 2009. A process that should have taken a couple of weeks was drawn out several months. My wife refused to allow the realtor to show the property. On September 11th, my attorney sent my wife's attorney an e-mail requesting that I be let into the house to pick up my belongings.

After several failed attempts my attorney was forced to write another e-mail. On September 14th 2009 my attorney sent my ex wife's attorney the following e-mail:

{"Apparently your client operates on her own schedule and in her own world: one where she does not appear to have to communicate with others and one in which she can do what she wants and have no consequences. She not only refused to answer calls over the weekend from the broker regarding the keys, she made sure she left the house with the keys on the kitchen counter (nice passive-aggressive behavior). Interestingly, I predicted it. Of course, she left piles of trash throughout so that not only does Alex need to get the yard spruced up, and move his things (of course, the TV, elliptical equipment and other gym equipment deemed to be his was not there), he now needs to clean the house. Further in spite of her statements for months that she has the title to his car, she does not have it now when it is vital to the closing. So since she disregards agreements that we've made, please be advised she will be responsible for one half of the short fall at the closing. Make sure she comes to the closing with a bank check payable to herself for $22,500.00. Make sure she plans to pay one half of the landscaping fees as well. As I heard from my client all weekend, my offer to pay to clean up the yard (expecting the yard merely needed mowing) is off the table."}

The yard had gone into disarray and the house began to look like a neglected foreclosure. To avoid splitting up our material possession my wife took it upon herself to pack up the house in its entirety and move out. All that was left was trash and a few of my personal possession that were smashed. I had to hire a landscaping company to come in and fix the yard. The grass and weeds had taken over and were creeping up to the bottom of the downstairs windows. Around $2,000 later, the house was habitable again. By this time property values were decreasing and it had become a buyer's market. I was forced to take a $65,000 loss on the house. As the divorce ensued, my relationship with my wife and her family had become so toxic that we could not be in the same room together. We had to have separate rooms at the closing to ensure everyone's safety.

At closing we were told that we were to both come with a check for our portion. As you can imagine, my wife and her father showed up with nothing and I was forced to clean out my bank account and part of my parent's to pay the $35,000. To add misery to disaster, while at the closing my father in law thought it would be funny if he stood outside the room I was in and dangle my son in front of me like he was a prize. All the while yelling, "Hey Alex don't you want to see your son? Come on out and see your son, Alex?" I strongly disliked that man and if I was mentally stronger, I am sure a fight would have broken out right then and there. The medication that the doctors had put me on allowed me to make it through high stress situations, but it took away my ability to function normally. I sat in my seat in a daze doing exactly what was asked of me by my realtor. I was there physically, but somewhere else mentally. Looking back, I can barely remember signing my name on the documents. I never want to be in that state mentally again.

~Chapter Twelve~

"To the world you may be just one person,
but to one person you may be the world."
-Brandi Snyder

Reaching Out

When I returned to MA, my doctor had encouraged me to reach out to old friends. I knew this was going to be a hard task. I had hurt so many people in my quest to make my marriage work. I broke friendships and hearts. I walked away when they needed me the most. I was scared to see if they would be willing to take me back with all my faults and apologies. I was about to find out if "I'm sorry" was enough. I knew of a few social networks that I figured could help me in my journey back to friendship. I decided to join Facebook.

Within a day, I had an influx of friend requests and I was overjoyed at the sight of it. I started talking to friends from college and high school that I hadn't seen in years. I was making plans and meeting back up with old friends that I had lost in the shuffle. On September 15th 2009 I checked my Facebook account and found an e-mail waiting for me. An old friend from college wanted to know if I would be interested in catching up over some coffee. Thinking back I really didn't know much about Marissa except that she had dated one of my friends all through college. I decided to keep pushing forward and made plans to meet up with her. I offered to pick her up because she lived one town over. I arrived at Marissa's parents' house where she was living at the time. I didn't find it odd in the least that a 29 year old was still living with her parents; hey, look at me, I was in the same boat. I walked to the door and she was standing on the porch waiting for me. As I looked around the room I could see a sea of pink and purple toys.

Me: "It's really good to see you."

Marissa: "It's good to see you too, I apologize for the mess of toys, they are my daughter's."

Me: "You have a daughter?"

Marissa: "Yes, is that ok?"

Me: "Of course! Actually I have a son."

Marissa: "You do? I didn't know that."

Me: "Well it looks like we have a lot of catching up to do."

We left the house and headed for a local restaurant. As we sat down at the table, we began to talk about how the years had treated us. I found out that I was not the only person in the world who was divorced or getting divorced. The more we talked, the more I wanted to listen. Our stories, our lives, were so similar. After we finished eating, I dropped her off and we said our goodbyes. Deep down I hoped to be able to talk with her again. I had never felt so connected to someone before. A few days later I called her to see if she wanted to go for a walk and talk. "I would love to!" She said. Our walks became more frequent, and our talks became longer and more detailed. I understood her and she understood me. Both of us needed each other's friendship and an unspoken understanding that neither one of us wanted anything more than that. Weeks began to pass and our friendship started to grow deeper. She was in the process of buying a town house, and I was in the final stages of divorce.

Months passed and I found myself seeking more time with her. She was so easy to talk to and I felt comfortable telling her my thoughts and feeling. At the time, I was working in a job that I disliked, and, now that winter had hit, sales started to drop. I was walking door to door in the freezing cold selling cable for Comcast. Things were getting bad and somehow she always managed to help me see the big picture, or the light at the end of the tunnel. I needed her more than ever. Our friendship grew into a relationship without us even realizing it. I found myself staying at her place three or four times a week. We would stay up all hours of the night talking and telling stories of the past. Communication and honesty were our greatest tools for survival as a couple. We told one another everything. We shared so many common interests, so many of the same loves. Our relationship was the kind that people wished for.

As time passed, I could feel myself slipping in and out of depression. I was on a multitude of medications, and because of it my memory was shot. We worked together to get through every obstacle that court and work had to offer. I never had to look for love and comfort, it was always there waiting for me. I felt like I was being saved by her and destroyed by my ex at the same time. I kept telling her that if I could get through this divorce, I would be stronger and healthier, I would be myself again.

I found myself in and out of court constantly. My ex wife was always late or she just didn't come at all. She refused to be flexible with switching days and adjusting times for my parenting time. I never got any holidays, not even Father's Day. I did my best to fight for more time, but the court never seemed to rule in my favor. On my weekly dinner nights, Marissa and I would pick up the kids and take them to my parents' house for dinner. It was a very uncomfortable situation for my parents, because my ex wife had made false allegations against my father involving Hanna. My ex-wife later denied making any such allegations; however the damage had already been done.

I was still living between my parent's house and Marissa's house, and my court appointed visitation allowed me to take both children for dinner, but I could only have Alex on the weekend overnights. I found it to be difficult to have both kids at the same time. At that time, Hanna was eight, and Alex was two. Hanna had to be watched at all times, like all siblings, they argued and disagreed over everything, but Hanna was a lot older and sometimes forgot how little Alex really was. She also liked to report information back to her mother that most of the time was not accurate or true.

This put a strain on my relationship with my son, and we decided as a family that I should relinquish all parenting rights to Hanna. I asked my lawyer to write up the papers and I gave up all legal and physical rights to Hanna. I was however, required to continue to support her financially, which seemed only fair since her biological father never did. I was broken up, and still am, over the decision I had to make. It was not one made lightly. I often think about what might have happened if I hadn't done it. I can honestly say that it was a decision that had to be made for the good of both children and it has brought my son and I much closer.

~Chapter Thirteen~

"Just when you think it can't get any worse, it can. And just when you think it can't get any better, it can."
-Nicholas Sparks

Legally Divorced

My divorce was finally official on November 9th 2009. I had walked away with nothing but the shirt on my back. Massachusetts guidelines forced me to keep her in the same standard of living that she was accustom to, a life that no longer existed. When I was terminated from Liberty Mutual, I was making $150,000. When I started at Liberty, I was making $35,000 a year. I worked long and hard to build up my book of business and clientele. By the time I met my ex wife I was finally making good money. I made $94,000 in 2005, $122,000 in 2006, $150,000 in 2007. Now I was working for Comcast selling cable door to door in residential areas and the starting salary was $35,000 plus commission. Due to my past sales experience and history, my ex-wife's attorney slated me to make between $70,000-$80,000 a year.

Taking this into consideration the judge, and both attorney's came to a set child support agreement of $425.00 per week with $100.00 per week in alimony. So I had to come up with $525.00 a week to pay my ex wife. I was not only paying for the kids, but my ex was allowed to factor in the rent that she was paying each month for her apartment while I was back home with my parents. My ex-wife was also able to get all the furniture, bank account money, and holiday time with our son.

Shortly after our divorce was final, on November 27th I received a phone call from my ex wife before my scheduled parenting time. She called to let me know that Hanna had driven over Alex's leg with her bike and had broken it. Alex was in a cast up over his knee. My instructions were to carry him everywhere and to not let him put any weight on it. I found out later that this incident had taken place on the 23rd and I was never notified. Per the court order, I should have been able to be present at the hospital with her to make any important decisions regarding our son. This became an ongoing pattern. Rules meant nothing to my ex-wife. For example, parenting time was set by the court, but my ex rarely showed. After every disappointing no show came another disappointing day in court. And each time nothing happened. How many verbal warnings can one person get before something happens to them?

As weeks passed, so did the holidays. I found myself hiding out. The thought of Thanksgiving and Christmas brought nothing but pain and anguish. Lying in bed on Christmas Eve I decided to share my New Year's resolution with Marissa. I was going to finally leave Comcast and get a better job, one that I could make a career out of. By the look on her face, I could tell that this was a great plan. However I could tell that she had some reservations. "Are you sure that you are ready mentally and emotionally for that?" She asked. "I know I'm not one hundred percent right now, but I can't live like this anymore," I said. I woke up at the crack of dawn and headed back to my parents' house to sleep Christmas day away. The next morning I began sending out my resume.

A month later, I got a call from a company named Cintas. The company was looking for sales representatives to sell their products to local businesses. All the signs pointed to yes, so I decided to go for an interview. I was offered the job and started on Feb 14th 2010. The job wasn't everything I had hoped it would be. My boss was a young, enthusiastic manager with a lot of promise. He reminded me a lot of myself and what I used to be. His "Rah Rah" attitude was over the top, and it showed his inexperience. I felt I was expected to do better than the rest because of my sales background. The amount of pressure and expectation was building and I was starting to think I made the wrong choice. I started to think that maybe the sales profession "flame" inside me was flickering out, after all how is someone suppose to get excited to sell toilet paper and soap? Why couldn't I get passionate about selling cable and now toilet paper and soap products? I could sell insurance like nobody could, so why was I struggling so badly?

When I started, I was given a $45,000 salary with no commission for six months. I asked my ex-wife if I could temporarily lower my child support until I could cover the payments again when the commission dollars kicked in. Her response was, "Too bad, Alex. Why don't you get a second job! And if that's not enough to cover the support payments then you can try for a third." I wasn't surprised by her answer, but I had no way to cover the payments. I was literally making $554.00 per week after health and taxes were taken out, and paying her $525.00 per week, leaving me with nothing. I was told that I couldn't go back to court to change my child support for three years after the divorce. Plus I had no money for an attorney. I had to seek more help financially from my parents. I later come to learn that I could have taken her back to court at any time to change the payment amount. Once I got wind of this informa- tion, I found an attorney and filed for a modification in child support, as well as multiple contempt accounts for no shows and late arrivals. I refused to live that way any longer. I refused to bleed my parents dry financially.

~Chapter Fourteen~

"In any moment of decision, the best thing you can do is the right thing; the next best thing you can do is the wrong thing; and the worst thing you can do is nothing."
-Theodore Roosevelt

The Fight

As I was dealing with work, my personal life was spiraling out of control. My ex had a new boyfriend who was nothing but trouble. He was the tough guy type, one that couldn't keep his mouth shut. All our pickup and drop offs were at the Plainville police station for the safety of both parties involved. On February 21st 2010 I was dropping my son off at the police station when her boyfriend got out of the car and began to approach me with the intention of taking Alex from me. I started to walk past him to hand Alex to my ex when he pushed me. My dad was in the car with me and he grabbed him and pulled him away from Alex and I. I put Alex on the ground and he ran to his mother, while I ran to get her boyfriend off of my father. By this time, the boyfriend had grabbed my father and thrown him to the ground, and was punching him repeatedly. I grabbed him off of my father and threw him onto the hood of my car. My father began to take a swing when my ex rushed over and kicked me in the back of the head so that I would let him go. That ended the altercation. My dad was bleeding from his eye where his glasses had broken and his face was badly bruised. It was decided that he should be taken by ambulance to Norwood Hospital. No one pressed charges, and the boyfriend was instructed by the police to stay away from the pickup and drop offs.

A few days later, I received a call from DSS. I found out that the police were mandated to call them because of the altercation that took place in front of the children. We each had to have a representative from DSS come to our house. Each of us was interviewed, as well as the family members we were living with, to make sure that it was a safe environment for the children. Everything went fine and we were able to continue with our scheduled visitation. My ex was finding it harder and harder to make it to the drop off and pickups on time. We would be waiting for 30-45 minutes for her to show up, which would cut into my visitation time. I found myself going to court (again!) and filing a complaint for contempt for late drop offs or no shows. This was taking a toll on me and my relationship with Marissa and my parents. We were both fed up with the games, and because of the altercation that took place, we couldn't send anyone alone to the pickups or drop-offs.

Now that I was working at Cintas, the pickup times were not convenient for me because I didn't get out of work until after five and I had to pick-up my son at 4:30p.m. My ex wasn't flexible, and if I had to cancel a day, she would not let me make it up, regardless if she had plans or not. It was becoming harder and harder to see my son and at the same time I was barely able to cover the child support. My entire paycheck was still going to my ex. I found myself in the red each month, not to mention that I couldn't even pay my own bills. I finally received a date to go back to court for a child support reduction and to change up the visitation to better suit my new schedule at work. I was able to lower my support from $525.00 a week, (which was $425.00 plus a $100.00 in alimony) to $425.00 a week (which was $325.00 plus $100.00 in alimony.) This left me with $200.00 a month for bills and expenses. My ex-wife won and the judge allowed the pickups and drop-offs to be at her house. The judge hoped that this would alleviate her from being late. I knew this was a bad idea, but my hands were tied. Not only was she still late to her own house, but now she was required to place Alex in my car. Not only was this a horrible idea, but it gave her the freedom to run her mouth off every time she placed him in his seat. One comment lead to another, and back to court we went.

~Chapter Fifteen~

"Drugs are not always necessary,
but belief in recovery always is."
-Norman Cousins

Cape Cod

I was allowed to have Alex for one week in July, and one week in August, per the parenting agreement. Ever since I was a child, my parents took us to Cape Cod, MA for a few weeks during the summer with the money they had saved up during the year. Now that I am older, my parents were nice enough to schedule their vacation around the weeks that I had Alex with me. July of 2010 was the first time I had Alex for more than a weekend. I was scared out of my mind at the thought of something happening to him. I was always on eggshells with him. The fear that he might get hurt while in my care, and my ex-wife's reaction, was always on my mind. As the week increased, so did my anxiety. I had no idea why I was feeling like this. I finally had my son for a whole week of uninterrupted time, and all I could think about was what if he gets hurt, what if he gets a sun burn. So many needless thoughts ran through my mind. Not to mention that I was constantly tired. I was overwhelmed and not sure that I could take care of him for an entire week. I was still not fully back mentally.

I was put on a number of medications for my anxiety from my doctor. The mixture was a disaster waiting to happen. I felt like sleeping all day, every day. I was extremely tired and out of it. I honestly didn't know if I was coming or going. I couldn't remember anything. I was scared. I turned to Marissa for help and support. She was great with kids and took on the roll of mom without even being asked. I thanked her every day for her help.

As the end of the week approached, I found it harder and harder to get out of bed. I didn't want to do anything or go anywhere. I was so depressed and I didn't know why. I finally had my son, and I was on vacation with my family and all the people I loved and cared for. What was wrong with me? It's amazing what anxiety can do to a person. I was so busy worrying that something bad was going to happen to him that would cause me to lose him, that I wasn't even able to stop and enjoy the time I had with him. When my week was over we drove back to drop Alex off to his mother. I can still remember the feeling of relief that came over me when we arrived back to the drop off safe and unharmed. I knew at that moment that things had to change. I wasn't going to let this person force me to live in fear. Fear of losing my son, fear of getting a better job, fear of having to give her every last cent I made. I was finally done.

When Marissa and I arrived home, I sat down to catch up on my e-mails and Facebook messages. I noticed that I had a Facebook message from my ex-wife's boyfriend. I was shocked! I had no idea what he could possibly want from me or how he even found me online. His message read as follows:

{So me and your ex-wife are no longer together because all she wants is a paycheck so I have some info you may want to know. If you are interested message me your cell number and I'll give you a call and let you know what she is up to.}

Why did he want to talk to me now? Why did he want to help me out? I started to think that maybe it was a set up. Maybe he was fishing for information for my ex-wife. Why would the guy who wanted to beat the life out of me in a police station parking lot want to chat like we were old friends? I asked Marissa what I should do. We talked it over and decided to give him my number. Marissa warned me not to give him any information about myself, just to listen to what he had to say, no agreeing or disagreeing with him. I thought that was a good idea. When he called he had a few things to tell me about the kids and the way she parented them. He also wanted to tell me about how my ex-wife treated him. He confided in me and understood where I was coming from. His story was so similar to mine I couldn't believe it. I thanked him for the information and hung up the phone. I had no idea if the stuff he was telling me was the truth or not, but it seemed so similar to what she had done to me that it was hard not to believe him. I took his information with a grain of salt and moved on.

~Chapter Sixteen~

"Thinking is the hardest work there is, which is the
probable reason why so few engage in it."
-Henry Ford

Downward Spiral

I was still not able to make the child support payments, and my parents were running out of money to
help me make ends meet. I was paying child support
money I wasn't making anymore. By this time I was on
the road daily with my job, driving all over Massachusetts and Rhode Island. On the 9th of August, on the way
to a client meeting, I got into a car accident on Route 95.
A truck was driving down the on ramp in front of me
when it dropped a rock larger than a softball out of the
back. The rock hit the ground and shattered sending large
pieces of debris toward my windshield. I swerved toward
the breakdown lane to avoid the rocks. In doing so I
smashed into a cluster of orange construction barrels. I
looked up to see a smashed windshield. I had an
overwhelming pain in my chest, and I thought I had

broken my sternum. I went to the doctor and found out that I had some internal bleeding. As they looked further they discovered that my esophagus was severely eroded, and I was just days away from a full-blown ulcer. The stress and anxiety from my divorce was literally killing me. I was put on a number of pain medications on top of the depression and anxiety medications that my doctors had me on. Due to the accident, I was out of work for a while and because of this they decided to let me go.

Marissa and I decided that I needed what we called a mindless job that wouldn't add any extra stress to my life. I found what I thought was the perfect job working for an infomercial production company. Unfortunately, it turned out to be the worst job I ever had. I was forced to read from a sales script, and if I deviated even a little they would take away my commission for that sale. I was frustrated and constantly getting in trouble for selling the products, but not following the sales script fully. Not to mention that I had to get up at three in the morning to go to a job where I had to ask permission to use the bathroom. I was in infomercial hell. I was the guy on the other end of the phone when you decided to purchase something ridiculous off the TV at 3 a.m. Everything about it was awful, and I quit after a month. Two weeks later, I saw on the news that the building's roof had collapsed from lack of snow removal.

Marissa knew I was spiraling down again mentally and I could tell she was getting scared. Our relationship was suffering and I was afraid I was going to lose her. I wasn't myself. I was tired, irritable, and I was secretly trying to self medicate. I contemplated giving my son up to stop the never-ending cycle of pain, depression and anxiety. Each time the thought crossed my mind Marissa was there to tell me that she supported whatever decision I made, but giving up on Alex was not an option, and I knew she was right. I was at the point where if something didn't give, I was going to self-destruct or put myself back in the hospital. I couldn't see the light at the end of the tunnel, and I was pretty sure I never would.

Rather than sending out resumes, I went out and walked business to business, personally delivering them, and was hired on the spot by a local hotel. I found myself a job working the front desk at the Marriott. I had to work nights, and once again, that interfered with my visitation schedule. I tried to take care of it and make the changes out of court, but, as usual, she refused to make any changes.

It was time for a change. I hired a new attorney to replace the last one that gave my ex-wife everything and left me with nothing. My parents were no longer able to help me make my monthly child support payments. I was broke, and the last thing I had left to my name was my car. I contemplated selling it, but then how would I get to work? My ex-wife's attorney told the judge that I was doing this on purpose, leaving job after job to screw my ex financially. With the help of my new attorney, the judge finally understood that I was broke. The judge looked me in the eye and said, "I believe that you are struggling, but if you are trying to hurt your ex, I will know." The judge put me on, what is called, temporary orders. My child support was finally dropped down to $212.00 per week and the alimony was wiped out. The judge told me that if I left my job at the Marriott, my child support would immediately go back up to $325.00 plus $100.00 in alimony. I prayed to whoever was listening that I could tolerate this job long enough to get myself back together mentally and emotionally.

The front desk at the Marriot seemed to be a good fit. I was making $9.00 an hour with no vacation time and no benefits. I was able to socialize with the guests, while providing service at the same time. This particular hotel served not only overnight guests, but long term residents. Bonding with some of the "regulars" made the time go by faster. A few weeks later, I decided to move in with Marissa and her daughter. The two of them would come at night and bring me dinner or just visit for a while. It was great to see them whenever I could. Now that I was working overnights we were on complete opposite schedules, but somehow we were able to make it work.

After I moved in with Marissa, my ex and her attorney demanded that they be shown pictures of the room Alex would be sleeping in. She also requested to sit down and have coffee with Marissa. Marissa wanted nothing to do with chatting over coffee, and frankly, I couldn't blame her. To my delight and surprise, Marissa did agree to a brief face to face at a local Dunkin Donuts. My ex wife took it upon herself to interview Marissa for ten minutes, asking questions that had nothing to do with the safety and well being of her son. After this it became a court order that we had to introduce significant others to the ex spouse. Three or four guys came and went out of my ex wife's house and I was never introduced to any of them. I thought to myself, "Why was it that when we were dating it take so long for her to let me meet her daughter, and now these men are coming to the pickups and drop offs?"

Christmas was fast approaching, and I begged my ex for visitation on Christmas Eve or Christmas day. I got, "no" for an answer to both. On December 25th 2010, around dinner time, I received a text message telling me that if I wanted Alex later that night I could pick him up at the police station at 7:00pm and return him the next day at 5:00pm. I looked at Marissa and she looked back at me with the same face of confusion. The woman who never gave me any time was asking me if I wanted to see Alex on Christmas night. I knew this was going to come with a price. I agreed to take him, and Marissa and I went to the station to pick him up. We backed into a parking space in the front parking lot at the station. My ex-wife pulled in and parked her car nose to nose with mine, leaving me no way to pull out. We noticed that my ex had her father with her, and when he got out of the car to get Alex from the back seat, Marissa decided it would be safer for her to get out and get Alex. Let's face it, her father wanted nothing more than to cause bodily harm to me. Marissa got out to grab Alex, but my ex-father in law stood in front of the car dangling Alex by one arm, yelling and waving his fists at me to "be a man" and get out of the car. Marissa tried to get Alex in her arms. Finally, he released Alex, and Marissa was able to get her and Alex into the car safely.

I thank God every day that it was winter and my car window was shut. As I turned to say hi to Alex, I heard a slam on my window. My ex-father-in-law was yelling and screaming vulgarities while spitting on my car window. All the while my ex was in the front seat of her car, laughing. This was nothing to laugh at. My son was being dangled by one arm in the freezing cold on Christmas night, and his grandfather was swearing and spitting at his father through a car window.

As my ex pulled away, Marissa and I went into the station to file a complaint. We asked why an officer never came out with all the yelling and commotion. Their answer was simply, "We didn't hear or see a thing." Apparently, there isn't a single camera overlooking the front or rear parking lots of the station. Information that would have been good to know for the past year, seeing how that was the sole reason for doing the pickups and drop-offs at the police station. That was a night I will never forget. It took everything in me not to get out of that car to protect my son and Marissa. I could tell by Marissa's face that I needed to stay in the car, because she knew I would have probably ended up getting myself arrested.

I thank her every day for the strength she had to stand out there in front of a raving lunatic. The police were good enough to drive over to my ex-wife's house to confront my father in law for his actions in the parking lot. He claimed that he was upset with me because I never paid my child support, and that spit must have come out of his mouth when he was yelling. Marissa and I had to laugh. I had never missed one child support payment, and I had every canceled check to prove it. It's amazing what people will say when confronted for their behaviors. The pickups and drop-offs as a whole were getting more ridiculous by the second. It got to the point where Marissa and I had to change Alex out of my ex wife's clothes and into our own, and then back into her clothes when we returned him. If, after a weekend visit, he came back in one of our outfits, she would threaten not to take him until we took him home and changed him into her clothes or she would throw our clothes away.

My ex was living a life that she couldn't afford. My ex-wife was living in an apartment that she couldn't afford. She was living beyond her means, and that always seemed to be my problem to fix. I was done. I had no more money to give, because she already had it all.

On February 24th 2010, my mom went to pick up my son for me at the police station. My ex was, again, a no show. The officer called my ex wife and asked her when she would be arriving for the drop off. My ex told the police officer that she had told me that she wouldn't be coming. My mom left the station, and later my ex-wife arrived at the station to inform the officer that she was not going to comply with the current probate order for visitation involving her son. My ex wife was advised that if she feels that the probate order is too difficult to follow then she would have to get it amended, but if she refused to follow the order criminal charges could follow.

~Chapter Seventeen~

"Do what you can, with what you have, where you are."
-Theodore Roosevelt

Enough is Enough

Life went on, and weeks at the Marriott continued to pass. I can remember telling Marissa that I really enjoyed the job; it was my boss that was making it hard to tolerate. I felt as though she was targeting me. I could never do anything right. With little to no training by her, I set out to figure it out on my own. Sure I wasn't perfect, but I was doing the best I could with what I had been trained in.

One night in February, I was working the desk when a gentleman came in asking about transportation for him and his co-workers. My manager had set them up to be transported by our van to their conference at 8:00am the next morning. I knew that the van was not available, because the inspection sticker had expired. My boss was on vacation, and she had left orders for the van to not be driven. Unbeknownst to me, she did not want this message relayed to the gentleman. I told him we would secure another mode of transportation for him and his staff. I called my boss to find out what she wanted me to do about a new form of transportation. My boss told me she would handle it. Before I could tell the guest, he called his boss, who in turn called me regarding the transportation issue before my General Manager could get a hold of him. I gave the Regional Manager on the phone my General Managers cell number, because she told me she wanted to take care of the situation. Later, I got a call from my general manager, and she was furious at me. The next day I was told to take a two-day leave of absence without pay. On the third day, I called my boss to get my schedule and she notified me that they were letting me go. I was in shock. I didn't know what to do. I asked to come in and to speak with her face to face and she refused. I immediately thought about court. If my ex-wife found out that I lost this job, my child support and alimony would go back up and I would be screwed. I was ready to throw in the towel. "Take me now officer" was all I could think of, because there was no way that I could make those payments.

I had to think fast. I went door to door to different local hotels looking to get hired. I sent out my resume everywhere. Now all I had to do was sit back and wait. Easier said than done, I told myself. I was going out of my mind worrying about bills and child support and anything else you could possibly think of. I couldn't shut my mind off. Sleep was no longer an option, and I found myself planning. I thought about writing a book, going back to life coaching, or teaching at local colleges again as an adjunct professor.

All that faded when, a week later, I heard from the Holiday Inn in Mansfield. They were looking for a sales manager. Clearly I had never worked anything but the front desk, but they knew I could handle the position with all my prior sales experience. After multiple interviews and another week of waiting, I was hired on March 4th, 2011. During the few weeks that I was unemployed, Marissa's family had been planning a trip to Disney World over April Vacation. We were invited to come, but we knew that money was extremely tight. Marissa's parents offered to pay our way and wouldn't take no for an answer. We were so excited. On the day I was hired, I notified them that I had a vacation planned for April, and they told me that was fine. I was relieved. I was so afraid they would say no and who could blame them. I was asking to take a vacation five weeks into a brand new job. Luckily, they understood that this was a preplanned vacation and they allowed me the time off. I notified my ex wife that I wanted to take Alex to Disney World during school vacation week in April 2011. Her first reaction was of course "No." So I decided that this was the last straw. I contacted my lawyer and told her that I wanted to file for full custody of Alex.

When I filed for full custody my ex-wife pushed for a full trial. It was at this point that my ex-wife's attorney notified my attorney that she had to conduct a deposition, which is a series of questions asked by the opposing council. My deposition was done in my ex-wife's attorney's office. I can remember sitting there and having questions fired at me. "Mr. Bering, did you have any romantic relations during the time that you were living with your wife?" "No." Most of the financial questions I could not answer because they dated back to 2005. Most were personal questions about my relationship with Marissa, both past when we attended college together, and present. Others involved the selling of properties and money trials. I was struggling to remember dates and figures off the top of my head, so they were forced to stop after three hours. I was told by one extremely agitated attorney that I better go home and find all the dates, facts, and figures to the questions that I could not answer, and to make sure that when I came back next time I was better prepared. I thought to myself how can you be prepared if you have no idea ahead of time what questions you will be asked? The deposition from those three short hours was typed out and totaled 154 pages. Communication between my lawyer and my ex-wife's lawyer stopped after a few weeks. By that point my family and I were out of money and I had to drop the custody battle. My ex-wife's lawyer stopped returning phone calls and e-mails and the deposition never went any further.

Weeks passed, and finally my lawyer was able to get my ex wife's lawyer on the phone. We were still waiting on a response to the trip to Disney, which started this whole thing in the first place. We also needed a signed letter that stated that my ex-wife was "allowing" Alex to go. Without that letter, she could potentially call the police on me for kidnapping, if in fact I took him out of the state without her permission. My attorney drafted the letter for her to sign. I was also forced to send her a full itinerary for the week with hotel information included.

I couldn't understand why my ex-wife could take my son wherever and whenever she wanted, and I had to get written permission. I did what was asked of me, and still, weeks later we had no answer. Two days before we were due to leave, Marissa was handed a signed letter at the drop off. Alex could come. We were so excited and angry at the same time. Because she had waited so long to sign the letter, we were not able to get flights and were forced to make the 22 hour drive to Florida. At that point, we didn't care. We were so excited to be going to Disney World! After my depression/anxiety episode at the Cape, I was scared that it would happen again, but this time it would be in front of Marissa's family, not mine. To my surprise, I was fine. The best part was that my son and I got to experience Disney World for the first time together.

~Chapter Eighteen~

"The mind is its own place, and in itself can make a
heaven of hell, and a hell of heaven."
-John Molton

Should I stay or should I go?

The job at the Holiday Inn was a great opportunity for me. I was given the position of sales manager with my own office. I was so happy to finally have a place to put the few awards, diplomas, and pictures of my son that weren't destroyed. Life was moving fast, and so was the job. I was in uncharted territory, but the one thing I had going for me was that I could sell anything (I believed in) to anyone. I was working long hours and finding myself in and out of court again over no shows, late arrivals, and changes to the parenting plan. I was on overload and this was still taking a toll on my relation-ship with Marissa. I was working full time and paying every cent I had to lawyers, child support, and personal bills. I felt worthless, I wasn't able to support the one person I cared for more than anything else, and that was killing me.

My father instilled in me that I was to be the provider for my family, and that weighed heavily on my mind. I felt like a freeloader, a bum on the street, and frankly, I couldn't imagine what she saw in me and why she continued to stay with me. Marissa always said that she didn't care about money. I tried to explain to her that there was more to my sadness than the money, but I knew she couldn't possibly understand the inner workings of my brain. She worked hard for everything she owned and I loved her for that.

As weeks and months passed I found myself fighting away the thought of leaving her and moving back in with my parents. I couldn't live with the fact that I was in her house unable to contribute to a single bill. I wanted to make her life easier, and I felt as though I was making it harder. I felt like I was dragging her down. She would tell me time and time again that she loved me and that was all that mattered to her, but I couldn't see that. I wanted to give her all the things that she gave me. I wanted to give her love, support, respect, and happiness. I had so much on my plate that there was nothing left to give. Every spare second, dollar, and ounce of love was given to her. I felt as though it wasn't enough because deep down I knew I had so much more to give, but I was not mentally able to. I knew what I had to do for myself mentally. I just didn't know when or how to do it.

The summer months arrived, and because I was new at my job, I hadn't yet accrued any sick, vacation, or personal time. I knew I had my son for a week in July and August and I had no idea what I was going to do. My parents and Marissa offered to take him to the Cape for the July week. I agreed and was able to go down on the two weekends. While I was at home and Marissa was gone, I began to think about leaving. I wanted to stop hurting her, I wanted to pay my way, and until I could do that I couldn't live in her house any longer. I made the decision to move out. I also decided that I was pretty much killing her emotionally, and I broke off the relationship all together. She was devastated and heartbroken to put it lightly. I was too. I thought about her constantly, and it was during that time that I realized that I couldn't live without her. I figured out that when you care for someone that much, they find their way back to you and you to them.

We kept in contact through the mail deliveries and the occasional text message. I was able to get her to agree to have dinner with me, and that is when I was able to explain my reasoning behind why I did what I did. I knew she would understand because communication was always our strong suit, and I was right, but I didn't know how to be with her and still get through court and the plans I had for writing a book and starting my own company. She deserved so much more than what I had to offer her. My time was not my own and I was working long hours, and I knew that she deserved better than that. It wasn't until we sat down and talked about how I still needed time to heal, but knew we cared for each other. So we came up with a plan to work on the book together. She knew my story like it was her own. I created my business card and company logo, and I put together my coaching theories, PowerPoint presentations, and designed a website on paper. We were on a roll. I was feeling happy and strong for the first time in so long. I was going to the gym, and there seemed to be an end in sight with court. I was finally feeling like the old Alex, the one that I couldn't wait for her to see.

~Chapter Nineteen~

*"The truth is, unless you let go, unless you forgive
yourself, unless you forgive the situation, unless
you realize that the situation is over,
you cannot move forward."*
- Steve Maraboli

Game Over

I received the final court date, October 19th2011. I couldn't believe that this court battle might actually end. The judge made it perfectly clear that she was tired of seeing us and that we needed to settle this, and fast. My lawyer called to notify me that my ex wife finally agreed to the new revised parenting plan. My child support would remain at $212.00 per week. I would get Alex for holidays, Father's Day, and his birthday on a, every other year, rotating schedule. I was also given my visitation schedule that I requested, every other weekend, from Thursday to Sunday. Things were finally coming together, and frankly I couldn't believe it. I was in utter shock and amazement.

Court was always difficult for me. The sight of my ex wife and either her mother or father was always enough to cause me severe anxiety. Our track record from the past led me to believe that this would be an all day event. I brought my brother with me for support and a listening ear. I arrived at the courthouse at eight o'clock with my brother and lawyer. My ex wife arrived with her attorney and her father. Her father always felt the need to stare me down and point his finger at me like he was going to run across the room and punch me. As the proceedings began, my lawyer was given a list of demands that my ex wife did not agree to or that she wanted changed or she wouldn't sign the parenting plan. My lawyer and I were in shock. We had been in close contact for weeks with her lawyer, and never had any of these things been even mentioned to us. All that stood between me and parenting time with my son was a list of fresh demands. I was presented with an old excise tax bill from 2008 for $47.00 that she wanted a check for as well as a check for $212.00 for a child support payment that she claimed I missed. It was like she was putting the last nail in the coffin. I agreed to her terms and wrote out the checks. We signed the paperwork and left the courthouse. "It's finally over," I said to my brother in complete disbelief. In the back of mind I knew that it would never be truly over, but at least it was for now.

Walking out of the courthouse, I got this over-whelming feeling of relief and excitement all rolled into one. I was finally going to be able to do what I wanted to do. I had a new exciting purpose in life, and no one was going to stop me. Ever since I filed for divorce, people started coming out of the woodwork to tell me that they were thinking about divorce or in the process of getting a divorce. It's like when you buy a new car, then when you start driving it, you see it everywhere. I was the guy that my friends and strangers were coming to for advice and information. People couldn't believe what I had gone through after only a year and a half of marriage. Friends going through similar times began to say, "Hey you got A-L-E-X-ed" to one another. I admit I had to laugh, because the irony was I really did give just about everything I had, and I guess I did get "X-ed."

I looked around and realized that even though I was broke, I had the one thing that nobody could take away from me. I was going to make people's relationships better. I was going to take on a new chapter in my life. I had the love and support of Marissa and my family, and I was going to make my dreams of becoming the "The Y Guy" a reality. My life was just beginning; the life I wished for and was destined to live.

All through my life I had taken on the role of "The Y Guy" for a number of high school and college students who were headed down the path of self-destruction. I taught them that there was more to life than the one that they were leading. I helped them to better their personal and business lives, and when the time came, I helped them prepare for job interviews and career changes, and to live life to the fullest. I want to continue with that and to expand on it. I want to be a motivational speaker and help people understand why they do what they do. I want them to see through their, "own eyes." I want them to realize that only they know why they do what they do, and that once you change your thinking you change your life. Getting divorced saved my life by helping me to finally see through "my own eyes."

~Part Two~

"All of us are born for a reason, but all of us don't discover why. Success in life has nothing to do with what you gain in life or accomplish for yourself. It's what you do for others."
-Danny Thomas

"Life can only be understood backwards,
but it must be lived forwards."
-Soren Kierkegaard

The Y Guy

"No one that I have ever met enters into a marriage
planning to get divorced."

The two great laws of life are you are either growing or dying. When things stop growing, they begin to die. This is true of relationships and people. What's the best time to get divorced? It depends on a number of factors, right? I did not even entertain the idea of staying together the "second time" for the sake of the children. The word on the street is, people would much rather come from a broken home than to live in one. I believe divorce is a different experience for everyone, and most importantly for the children. My son and Hanna's take on divorce will likely be very different than mine, I'm sure.

To me, divorce was the only remedy to my unhealthy marriage. Divorce, when I went through it, seemed to be all around me. Although most people manage to get through this period of stress, a significant number of divorce casualties are the victims of murder, suicide, and madness. I learned that there is a wide spread belief in the divorce courts that men soldier themselves through this process and are not suffering, simply because they are not showing their emotions. Although I put on a brave heart and tried to believe that this wasn't affecting me, the reality was far different. For me, repression weakened my sense of self, and increased aggression, depression, and self-destructive behavior. Divorce put me right on the edge of sanity. I was falling over the edge and trying to numb the pain with medication, alcohol, and marijuana, which in turn was destroying me and my family. This wasn't the kind of pain that you could see like a broken arm or leg. This was internal pain that ate away at me emotionally, physically, and mentally. I needed to put the stigma of divorce behind me and move on.

It takes two to get married and only one to say, "I'm done!"

Once you fall into the pit of despair, it's hard to get out. I sought the help of therapists to answer my question "why?" Why was I suffering so badly? Why couldn't I put this behind me and move on? I realized that I was asking questions that they could not answer. "I don't know Alex, why do you think your marriage failed?" They would turn my question into a question, frustrating me more. Until, I realized, they hadn't seen or experienced what I had been living through day in and day out, so they couldn't possibly understand what it was like to walk in my shoes. I was searching for just one person who went through something similar to what I went through. Someone who survived divorce and could help me understand how I could survive mine. I kept coming up empty time and again.

I started to wonder if my story was to the point of unbelievable, as many people would say when they heard it. Asking these therapists for answers was like asking a smoker how to quit smoking. However, if you were to ask a smoker for advice on how to quit smoking, I am sure they could give you a number of suggestions. So why don't they quit if they have so many tools and advice to do so? It's the same as all the therapists. They had all the advice in the world, and I left the office and didn't know what to do with it. I had all these suggestions from therapists, lawyers, family members, and I was trying everything I could and nothing was working. Advice is great, but until you have gone through the process yourself and experienced what the other person has lived through, then advice is just that: a suggestion of what might work for you. There is a large gap between advice and help. It's perfectly natural for people to give advice, make suggestions, and want to help you. However, the only one who can help you is you. It's up to you to seek and find the answers to your never ending why's.

When I was growing up, my family had many games we used to play. My favorite was the "why" game. If you've been around children, you will encounter it at some point. The game gave me the opportunity and encouraged me to do some basic research to explore and find the best answers to my questions. This was my way of exercising my mind and helping me to seek out the best answers for myself. My never ending "why's" weren't meant to exasperate people; it was to answer the unanswerable. As a child I began to see, through *"my own eyes,"* an endless possibility of questions and to discover and develop intellectual and emotional intelligence. I began to make connections between cause and effect, which is why to this day, at 34 years of age, I am still asking "why." Some people don't respect the power of asking "why." In fact, sooner or later, we stop asking questions, and that is extremely unfortunate. Asking "why" seems so easy. So, why don't we ask "why" more often? Is it because we really don't want to know why something is happening, or why someone is doing what they are doing, or saying what they are saying? Maybe it is because we are afraid of the answer. Maybe we think it isn't worth the fight or aggravation.

After hitting "rock bottom," I want people to now understand why asking why is so very important. I want the word why to be the most honored word in our vocabulary. There has been way too much suffering, disagreements, and conflicts over the word why, and people need to learn how powerful the word really is. I wrote this book as the foundation of why people do what they do including me. Most of us know why we do what we do, the trick is letting others in on the secret. People who don't understand why they do what they do have no other choice but to go blindly through life. Being you is easy. The most difficult thing to do is to be what other people want you to be. Don't let them make you behave their way. Consider how hard it is to change yourself, and you'll understand what little chance you have to change other people. Every individual is unique and we should remember that rather than relying on limited stereotypes of men and women. So then, if it's not gender that accounts for the leading cause of conflict within relationships, then what is it? It's our experiences, communication, behavior, and lastly, our ignorance. If a relationship fails, we owe it to ourselves to find out exactly why it failed. It's not always you that may be the cause of the failed relationship. So look deep down inside and ask yourself "Why?"

Wouldn't you like to know why…….

Wouldn't you like to know WHY people do what they do? Let's think for a minute, why did you pick up this book? Stop for a second and ask yourself, "Why?" Only you know, consciously or unconsciously. I can assume I know why you picked up this book, but it is habit to assume. Often in life we see a behavior and begin to assume we know what is causing it without having any real idea of why. A perfect example of this is the story of the Jefferson Memorial. A few years ago, there was a big problem with bird poop at the Jefferson Memorial. It seemed to be a target for every bird in Washington, DC. Yes, the other Memorials got pooped on too, but the Jefferson was constantly covered, and the cleaning expenses were over the top, not to mention that the cleaning solutions were eating away at the Memorial. The park members assigned to the case began asking "why" the Jefferson memorial was covered in three times more bird poop than the others. An investigation was started, and they came to learn that birds love spiders, and the memorial was covered in spiders. It was covered in spiders because spiders love midgets (insects). And it was covered in midgets because they loved the light. Midgets like to procreate in areas where the light is just so. To fix the problem, they started turning the lights of the memorial on later in the evening so that the midgets would leave. When the midgets left, the spiders left, and when the spiders left, the birds left as well. So there you have a great example of the benefits of asking a series of why's to get to the root of the problem.

The bottom line is that conflicts in relationships come from a lack of communication and assumptions in behavior. We have two ears and one mouth, and the reason is that listening is twice as hard as talking. Poor communication is cited as the most frequent and serious cause of conflict. Drop the assumptions. Making an assumption is the mark of a lazy communicator. Never assume anything just because it is obvious to you or considered common sense. This is why, all too often, people make rapid judgments about the behavior of others such as good, bad, proper, or improper. The key here is to never assume why a person is crying, laughing, or expressing emotions. Only the person that is doing the behaving knows exactly why. This is why each person responds individually to the behavior of others. By behavior, I mean what is said or done, which others can see, hear, and then talk about. Think about it, how in the world can two people see the exact same thing, yet come away with two completely different views of what they saw? This is because we all see the world through our own eyes.

Times are changing with new technologies and information, but what about us? Are we changing? Have we changed our behavior throughout our marriage? Do we have a career, do we have children, are we making more money, did we lose a job, how do we behave? The answer is our behavior is continuously changing. We all know we begin learning and changing the day we are born, and continue till the day we die. Is learning a change in behavior? It's time to find out. We need to take the time to learn about ourselves, who we are, and why we do what we do. This might give us the insight we need to figure out why others around us behave the way that they do. In the end, divorce can teach us all something about ourselves, and others. Is your divorce a failure, or a new beginning? Once you figure out your why question, after all else fails, then it's time to ask me (The "Y" Guy).

The Y Guy
asktheyguy@yahoo.com